Divisible by 2

John Whiteman **Divisible by 2**

Commentary by John Hejduk

Chicago Institute for Architecture and Urbanism
The MIT Press
Cambridge, Massachusetts
London, England

A project of
The Chicago Institute for Architecture and Urbanism
The Skidmore, Owings and Merrill Foundation
1365 North Astor Street, Chicago, Illinois 60610
Board of Directors:
Thomas H Beeby
David M Childs
Henry N Cobb
Peter D Eisenmann
Frank O Gehry
Bruce J Graham
Michael Graves
Stuart Lipton
Charles W Moore
Harold Schiff
Robert AM Stern
Stanley Tigerman
Director: John Whiteman
Administrative Director: Sonia Cooke
Produced by the Publications Studio of the CIAU
Director of Publications: Richard Burdett
Graphic Designer: Mika Hadidian
Production Editor: Jane Allen
Studio Assistant: Valerie De Leonardis
Photographs: Margherita Krischanitz
and John Whiteman
Typesetting: Anzographics, Chicago, IL
Printers: Meridian Printing, East Greenwich, RI

Distributed by The MIT Press
Cambridge, Massachusetts and London, England

The publishers would like to thank
The Graham Foundation, Chicago, for a generous
contribution towards this publication.

Library of Congress Cataloging-in-Publication Data
Whiteman, John E. M.
Divisible by 2/ John Whiteman:
commentary by John Hejduk.
ISBN 0-262-73093-6 (pbk.)
1. Architecture, Domestic—Research.
2. Architecture—Political aspects.
I.Hejduk, John, 1929-. II.Title III.Title: Divisible by two.
NA7125.W48 1990
728'.092—dc20   90-6603
                    CIP

Contents

Introduction

The project Divisible by 2 was conceived as an architectural experiment. I decided to set at play certain cross-relationships between building, image and word. The building, perhaps it was a building, perhaps a model, could be re-calibrated to adjust its architectural effects. It existed as a machine which could calibrate and effect a spatial definition at the same time as it exhibited the machinery of its architectural operations.

Divisible by 2 has been described as a "machine for architectural emotion." These are the words of Bruce Graham, retired partner of Skidmore, Owings & Merrill. I wish to thank Bruce Graham for his trust. It is his extraordinary vision and persistence which has made possible The Chicago Institute for Architecture and Urbanism under whose roof and auspices the project was designed, manufactured and finally assembled off-site in Austria.

I would also like to thank Stanley Tigerman for seconding eight students from the School of Architecture at the University of Illinois, Chicago, to work on the project. My deepest thanks go the students themselves: Michael Ambrose, Madelaine Boos, Ann Clark, Ken Fougere, William Hornoff, Dan Marshall, Brett Roberts and Mark Searls. In the space of seven weeks they helped to design, detail, manufacture and assemble what until then had been but a vague and difficult set of ideas in my head. Finally I want to thank Dietmar Steiner and the Donnau-Festival of Lower Austria for inviting me to participate in the exhibition at St. Pölten.

The project was built as an examination of the political in architecture. It was shown at the Geburt einer Haupstadt (Birth of a Capital Exhibition) on the occasion of the moving of the state capital of Nieder-Ostereich (Lower Austria) away from the cosmopolitan scene of Vienna to the rural town of St. Pölten. Ironically, the building was destroyed by fire bombs on the night of Sunday, 28 July 1988. Although the building had stirred some local controversy, uniting both the political left and right in their dislike of it, it is not known who destroyed the building, or why.

The text that follows is an edited version of a diary which I kept during the design and construction of the building. It records in a chronological sequence my thoughts and preoccupations with the design. Broadly, it moves from intention to decision and description to reflection. Following my own text is a commentary by John Hejduk. Hejduk has written his own criticisms and concerns as a text in parallel to my own. His comments reflect the continued debate which we have concerning architectural theory and the production of artifacts. I wish to thank him for his care and advice.

JW Chicago July 1990

DAMEN

This building does n

0 Text and Building

HERREN

...nswer to the text.

0.2 It is not the case that this text articulates a line of inquiry

to which the building is the answer. The text does not interrogate

the building, nor explain it.

0.3 *Rather, the text and*
the building are different
ways of positioning
a line of work in the
same difficulties, of moving
(I don't want to say
'of asking questions')
in the same circuit
of tensions and oppositions.
A difference of medium,
that is the difference here.

0.4 *There is, however,*
a dependency of the
building on word.
This is consciously
signalled by the use of
false signs on the doors.

1 Beginnings and Motivations

1.1 The building is an attempt to understand and subsequently render the space and experience of architecture itself as political.

1.12 Perhaps this is a futile task. For maybe every act of building is inevitably political, being inextricably caught within the power system that brings a building into being. Yet surely there is a difference between an architecture that is reflexive of the author's consciousness of this fact and one that is not.

1.13 Perhaps there is no stable mechanism for the self-reflexion of the political in building. No mechanism which is historically stable can be recognized continually over time in durable form. In thinking the political in architecture, there is encountered constantly a twin problem of the embodiment of political meaning in architecture and the temporal stability of its subsequent recognition. Possibly it will not do to have framed the problem in this way: the prospect of embodied meaning and its recognition may initiate an intolerable burden, a task which can never be completed. The problem, as stated, may operate as a trap: the structuring of the problem itself being the greater problem.

1.14 And yet, I have the intuition that much of the architecture that I admire has confronted the question of its own political status. So what is at work in such buildings? Am I reading the failure of the attempt to register the political in building? Is failure ironically the only form of success to be had in such questions?

1.15 Can a political architecture, self-consciously construed, be achieved by a critical engagement of the difficulties inherent in the world that power is trying to put in place, and, at the same time, by a simultaneous reflexion of the difficulties of the way such a meaning can be represented or made manifest in building?

1.16 Or is there no difference discernible between the content of architectural meaning and the mechanism of its realization? To make a real world, one that is politically alive, must one rid oneself of the false puzzles of representation?

1.17 As Wittgenstein says, "(The question 'What do I mean by that?' is one of the most misleading of expressions. In most cases one might answer: 'Nothing at all — I say...')"[1] What can I do in response to such a question as "What do you mean by this?", but say or do it again? When you ask, "What does it mean?", do you want me to do something different?

1.18 Can we not enter a building without words?

1.19 Or is this line of thinking too purist, saying that sense can only be found here or there, in this medium or that? Is not the greater sense to be made in the play between senses, between different media of sense-making? Is the question of medium a dead end?

1 L Wittgenstein, *Zettel*, Berkeley, 1967, p 2e

1.2 Architecture and Human Difference:
The inscription of subjectivity in building

1.21 Architecture possesses a relation of ambivalence to human difference, to the differences at work in life. It makes a space for their play and perpetuation, in part even creates the fact of difference, but is itself withdrawn from the object of its influence, life. It is itself an inevitable but impossible neutrality. Architecture frames the differences of life but cannot participate in them fully.

1.22 The withdrawal, the apparent disengagement of architecture from life, may give rise to an illusion that architecture itself is somehow autonomous, or neutral, operating as our surroundings yet as a realm set apart. But, architecture, so it is said, can also be read as an index of the form of life which it frames, as an inscription of the subjectivity for which it was made. Is there a contradiction here: a pretense at neutrality and disengagement set against a reading of architecture as marked with life? In what conception could both sides of such a contradiction be understood as true, and the sense of contradiction thus diffused?

1.23 The act of withdrawal is the construction of an illusory neutrality. In withdrawal something about the operation of architecture, perhaps its influence in the construction of the subject, remains unacknowledged and is hidden from recognition if

not from view. Yet, in withdrawal architecture is somehow marked by the covert nature of its operations. The fact of withdrawal and the negative sense of marking, of being marked, give rise to the double sense of neutrality and subjective inscription. Thus is the sense of contradiction defused.

1.3 Can the political in architecture be awakened by an attack on the banality created through the functionalist attitude which so predominates everyday discussions about building?

1.31 The functionalist attitude to architecture makes of building a passive servant to our desire. Functionalist architecture, in the naive sense as Rossi defines it, is fundamentally the construction of a relation of dominance over an object.[2]

1.32 What does it mean to have an object which panders to our desire? What kind of relation between a person and an object is achieved in forcing subservience of things to human need or desire? An object passively construed as a service to life becomes banal.

1.33 The images of the banal can be used, when corrupted, to deflect expectations of the ordinary, thus awakening a more political sense of the object.

1.34 In this building the image of the lavatory is used as an attack on functionalism.

1.35 In the lavatory the door is (and has) a simple sign, indicating ease of access and certainty of use.

1.36 In the lavatory architecture is at its most abused.

1.37 In the banality of the lavatory door is subsumed the major system of devices by which architecture is appropriated in(to) life. The sign indicates function. The door, itself a metonym of the body, indicates passage and, in conjunction with the sign, ease of access. Door and sign together indicate a security if not a certainty.

The threat of the other side of the door is nullified by the exterior sign arousing a confidence of use, and in turn creating new threats of 'the other'. The ordinary door, upon opening, places the subject at the threshold of a room which by optical projection s/he can grasp as intelligible. A visual map is made of the room in a single glance. The projection once made, the architecture thus appropriated, the room can be used in accordance with its function. Nothing in the architecture is to trouble the subject further. The architecture is exhausted, no longer needed. It can be left behind, forgotten.

2 A Rossi, *The Architecture of the City*, Cambridge, Massachusetts, 1982, pp 46-48

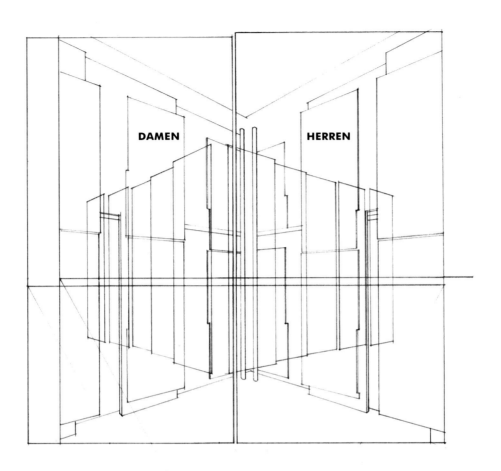

1.4 The pavilion is the essay form of architecture.
This building attempts to foil the systems of
architectural appropriation at work in the
banality of function.

1.41 It is also partly inspired by a parallel
observation in *Écrits* by Jacques Lacan.[3]
Lacan depicts a figure of two doors:
one marked for men, the other for
women. The figure occurs in a passage
where Lacan is discussing the failures of
nominalism in relation to the "agency
of the letter in the unconscious." He
intends by the example "to show how
in fact the signifier enters the signified,"
thus destroying by contamination the
distinction on which a nominalist
argument is based. The nominalist
denies the existence of entities labelled
by general categories and prefers to
speak only of individuals. His argument
for the existence of individuals turns on
the arbitrariness of names, their
independence from things and their
resemblances to each other. Lacan's
observation that name and thing,
signifier and signified, enter into one
another is intended to deny the
nominalist's argument by denying the
independence of name from thing.

1.42 This building announces its entrance
with two signs: DAMEN and HERREN.
But, the announcement is at once
significant and a herald of its own
futility and difficulty.

1.43 It is significant in the sense that the
building is a deceit which displays
itself at every turn.

1.44 The sign on the door is a common
device of indication in architecture.
It is used when architecture fails or
cannot itself be sufficient as an index.

In the lavatory the sign is commonly
used to separate the sexes more for
moral rather than hygienic purposes.
In this building the separation indicated
by the signs on the door is not fulfilled
on the interior.

1.45 The sign is the failure of architecture.
Architecture always fails?

1.46 Ironically, this building comes to
depend on signs, such as words, for
its understanding. In this instance
the dependency of building on word
is ironic because it was intended
originally to achieve their independence.

1.47 Intention in architecture forces a
dependency of building on word by
seeking a building form that is
accountable to its design intentions
verbally stated. Insofar as the
difference in medium between building
and word marks a gulf between sign
forms that cannot be negotiated

directly, an intention, stated verbally,
cannot be carried out on its own terms.
In a sense, intentions to build always
fail. However, this failure of intention
does not imply a corresponding
failure of the building. The building
may succeed on other terms, in other
ways.

1.48 In this line of thought I am led
to three other questions. First, what
is the possibility of tracing a line
between intention and building:
where is the thread lost? Second,
does this first question assume
intention to be exclusively verbal?
Third, if intentions are not merely
verbal, what relations and
contaminations are at work
between word and building?

3 J Lacan, *Écrits*, New York,
1977, p 151

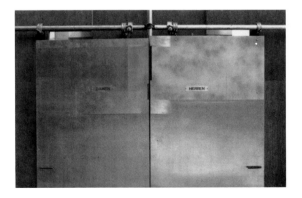

1.5 The building is a mechanism for the adjustment of architectural space.

This isn't the wind in the maples, my boy
No song to the lonely moon
This is the wild roar of our daily toll
We curse it and count it a boon
For it is the voice of our cities
It is our favorite song
It is the language we all understand
It will soon be the world's mother tongue

Bertolt Brecht,
Song of the Machines, 1925-28

1.51 It is constructed in such a way that the internal space of the building can be altered or disfigured by re-calibrating the structure manually with a set of wrenches. The columns can be raised or lowered by two feet. The panels will simultaneously be raised or lowered as the frame is moved. The panels can also move horizontally, parallel and perpendicular to the frame. The doors on the panels can be opened to make incursions into the room as calibrated. The way the space has been set or adjusted is disturbed on entry. The surface of the metal can also be distorted to bend the top and bottom of the interior surface of the wall into the room.

1.52 Once constructed, the building was indeed calibrated. The interior panels were set using deflections from the orthogonal which were sensible but not immediately noticeable. If a deflection drew attention to itself so that it was noticed right away, then it was diminished, re-calibrated to be a deflection that the eye could barely discern. The purpose of this criterion of 'the barely noticeable' was to pressurize a specific form with subliminal senses which are exterior to it.

1.53 The building can be set in many configurations, ranging from the subliminal to the overtly grotesque. Each setting could constitute not just an individual performance of the building, but perhaps a different architectural work altogether. It was

decided to set the building using only marginal deflections calibrated to be registered only subliminally.

1.54 As set, the deflections in the building produced the illusion of a redressed orthogonality to persons entering the building off-center through both doors. The interior was arranged so that the wall opposing entry was divided into two sets of surfaces, one set orthogonal to each of the divided entrants. The scale of these deflections was calibrated so that the wall could also be read as a single, albeit interrupted, plane.

1.55 The building is an experiment in architecture. It is as much a full scale model as it is a building. The fact of the building as an experiment has been registered in the architecture itself. The mechanism of the building has been rendered overt. That is to say, every rhetorical effect of the building has been underlined, as it were, by the exposure of the mechanism which produces that effect.

1.56 The concept of the building as an architectural machine was intended as part of the architecture (of the machine).

1.6 To make an object which is politically situated requires two transformations.

1.61 On the one hand, the experiencing subject must be moved, moved without force or deceit from the status of user to that of performer. On the other hand, the building itself must be made such that the power hidden in the banal is released. This disruption of the ordinary will trigger the transformation of the subject from user to performer. S/he must encounter the difficulties created by a disturbance of the ordinary.

1.62 And must this be counted as a deceit? To disturb the ordinary?

1.63 The interesting question to ask of the ordinary is, How did it get to be that way? Why do we regard something as ordinary and something else as not? Should we speak of ordinations rather than 'the ordinary'?

1.64 The ordinary is not something that is simply given. It is a constructed affair; hence, the conjoined root and the double senses of 'ordination' and 'ordinary'. Invoking the constructional aspect of reality, the association of 'the ordinary' with the term 'ordination' implies that the ordinary is not merely something to be passively accepted but that it is something about which we can have some choice and over which we can exercise some intelligence and determination. Worlds are made as much as found.

Doors

ordinary door is a curiously discordant device. When closed, its full
ace operates in the memory as a recollection of the absent figure. But in
only a part of the doorway serves for the passage of the body. The body
ses through the door off-center, towards the leading edge. The edge, which
nged, is clear of the passage of bodies. Doors are always disfigured.

2.11 This is so in the sense that there is an incongruency between the figure of the door as remembered (closed, presented orthogonally, and posing as a figure in a centralized presentation) and the figure of the door in use (opened, presented obliquely, the figure passing off-center at the leading edge of the door).

2.12 This building starts from a figure of two doors. The doors open outwards with the leading edge away from the center of the facade. For a symmetrical facade the doors are hung the wrong way. There is an announcement made on the doors of an impending (already expected) division of the sexes. But the division is only valid at the threshold. Perhaps not even then. In the interior the sexes are not in fact separated. There is but a single space. On the interior one is in the presence of the 'other' (sex). The fact that the division of the sexes implied by the doors is not fulfilled in the interior of the building is simultaneously registered on the very doors which make the announcement in the first place. The doors act as titles for the building, for they are analogous to its plan.

The door handles index
the difficulties expressed in
the building. They are set
too close to the surface. When
using the handle, the hand brushes
the metal surface of the door.
The space between door and
handle is too narrow.

2.13 The figure of the two doors taken together is composed both as a division and a unity. The interior of the building, the fact that it is a single, undivided space, is reflected in the unitary aspect of the composition of the doors. When closed, the metal surface of each individual door is presented so close and coplanar with the surface of the adjacent door that the two doors together take on the appearance of a single sheet. Elements such as signs and markings are placed on each door so as to emphasize the union of the two and not their separateness. This emphasis is done quietly, without announcement, and in the manner of an abstract painting.

2.14 The doors present externally and literally the discrepant dimensions of men and women as registered in the *American Graphic Standards*. The doors are marked, scratched, burned, inscribed, at points which correspond to points of vulnerability on the human body: knees, genitals, stomach, breasts, eyes, head. The figure for each door is not coextensive with its own dimensions, but relies instead on a portion of the other for its own composition.

2.15 The doors are presented as discordant and are without any frame. They are hinged on vertical pins at the top and bottom. The hinges are not aligned with the inside edge of the door. Instead the hinges are spaced so that, when both doors are open, a space equivalent to that of a body is revealed. This space cannot be occupied. It is already occupied by the neutrality of the center column. When the doors are open and in use, the presentation of sexual difference on the facade disappears, since it would then be redundant given the presence of actual bodies. In one sense this can be said to have already happened in the external composition of the doors, which in the design of their surfaces blur the sexual distinctions that they so blatantly announce.

2.16 When the doors are closed the dimensional difference of the sexes is given in the overall dimensions of the doors. In relation to the simple harmonic proportions of the frame these dimensional differences read as discrepancies. The doors are placed as a discordant composition in an otherwise harmonic facade.

2.17 Once the door is opened, direct access to the interior is foiled by the presentation of a metal surface, the leading edge of which bifurcates the line of the approaching body. The expectation of direct and convenient access is aroused by the presentations of the sign on the exterior. The foil of the metal arrests the expectation of access. Entry into the building is easy, but requires that the entrant move away the sheet of metal presented against the body, much in the manner that a domestic screen door must be negotiated as a second closing or opening. The act of opening the sheet of metal as an inner screen door places the body at the operative point of illusion on the interior.

2.18 The space in the wall is dimensioned to be the space of a body. It reveals most fully the machinery of the illusions concerning perspective in the interior, and the relations between the layers of articulated surfaces which comprise the building. The mutual distance between the building's surfaces and their supports is clearly revealed. The frame ironically is not stable without the presence of the panels which it ostensibly supports.

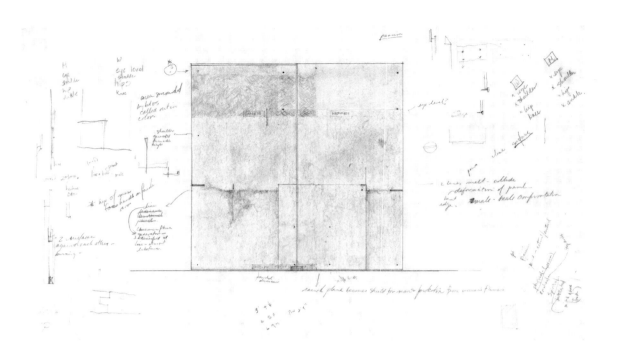

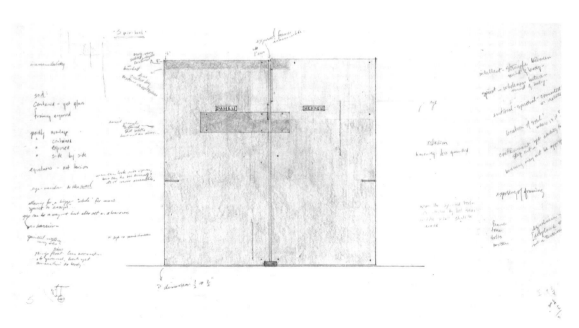

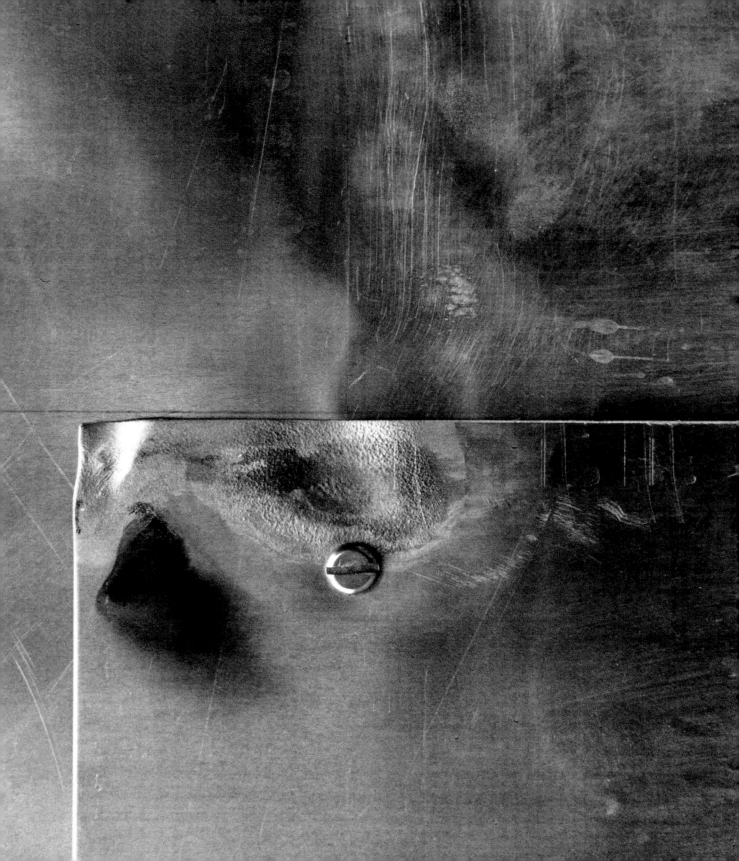

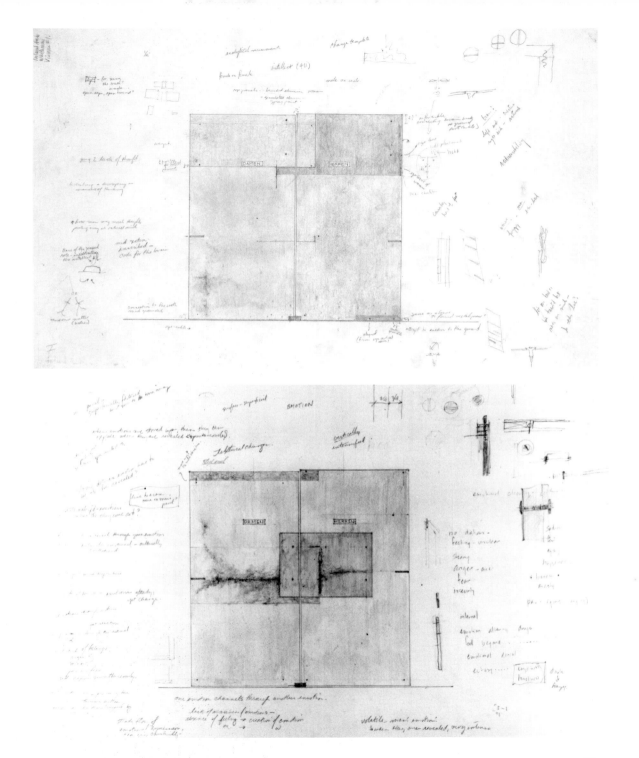

2.2 The Plan

2.21 The plan of the building is based on a perfect square. No construction above the floor is allowed to touch or occupy this square.

2.22 The width of the building is equal to three times the width of the figure of the doors. A pair of lavatory doors is placed centrally on all four sides. The plan of the building therefore becomes a 9-square grid, a mandala form, a traditional inscription of the city. The space of the city is fundamentally the space of the 'many' not the space of 'one'. It is the space of the 'We' not of the 'I'.

2.23 The central square of the mandala is not occupied and is further voided by the construction of experience on the interior, which becomes aimless.

2.24 The frame is not allowed to occupy the corners. Columns at the corners are doubled, being offset from the corner, each by 5 inches. The column at the center of the elevation is partially hidden by the door.

2.25 The five panels of each wall are arranged on a curve which, in combination with the opening sections of the panels on the interior, set up a mechanism for the correction of the building's perspective. The intention is as follows: the device of the doors separates the sexes one from another; each must enter off-center to the square of the building. The wall opposing each pair of doors is calibrated so that not one but two surfaces may be read. One surface is orthogonal to the entrant, creating the illusion that s/he is back on center. But this effect is immediately disturbed by the presence of the second surface which creates the same effect for the entrant through the door not taken, the door of the other sex. The illusion creates a hesitation in moving forward.

2.26 This illusion, although intended as 'weak', does not function in the way anticipated. The greater hesitation is caused by the mechanism of the door itself, the baffle. The illusion, if noticed, passes quickly over into a rotational experience of the body in the interior.

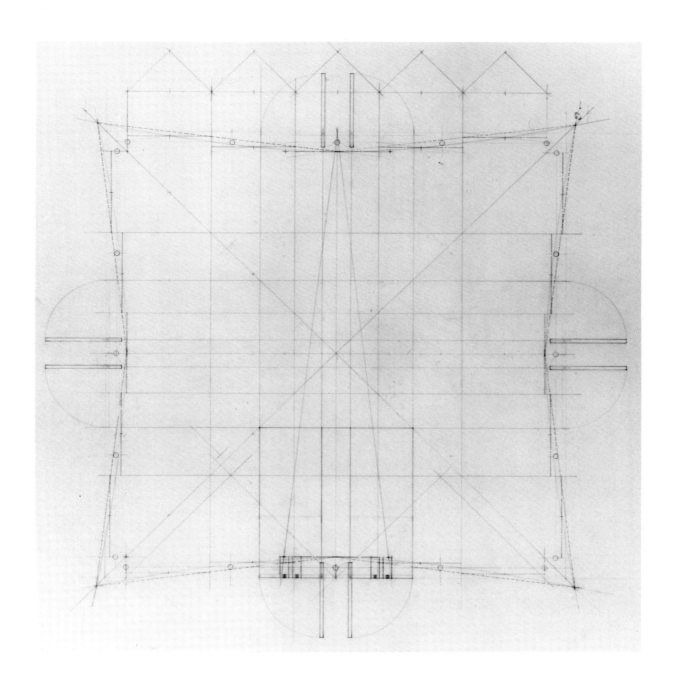

31

2.3 The Interior

2.31 On the interior no harmonic proportions are allowed.

2.32 The interior presents discordant walls from which the occupant tends to turn away. But turn away from one, and another wall is immediately encountered. Turn away again, and the rotational sense of the interior becomes activated. But this activity leaves one at the center which quickly becomes too painful to occupy. Mostly, persons seemed to settle away from the center, near a corner and close to the walls so that their projective effects are diminished.

2.33 The experience of the interior is available in movement, when the discordant dimensions cease to be read as such and become simple concatenations across different reflective surfaces.

2.34 The interior rhythms of the building are created entirely from the discrepant dimensions between men and women. These rhythms are carried in two tiers of panels abstracted from the doors. They form a hall of metonyms of the body, and are cast over with the matt sheen of a vague mirror, the granular speculation of the surface of the aluminum.

2.35 On entrance to the interior the central panel closes in the wake of the passage of the body to create the closure of a hall of mirrors. The hall of mirrors has been used repeatedly by others as a metaphor of the difficulties of our subjectivity. It is used here despite all threats of repetition.

2.36 The section is determined by taking a cone of attention and extending it across the dimension of the square to the wall opposing entry.

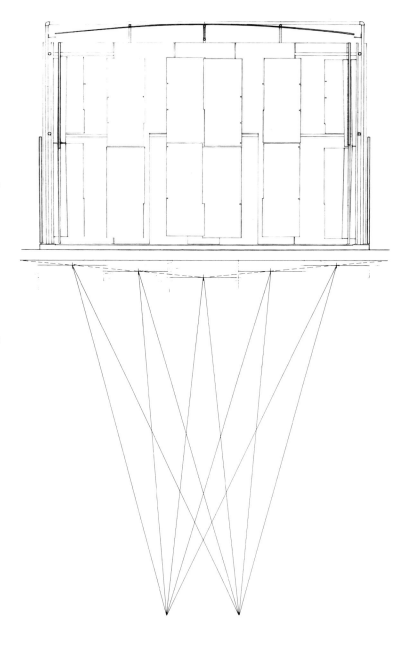

2.4 The Facade

2.41 The facade departs from a series of classical harmonies. These are presented in the same sign-like manner as the signs on the doors. Their direct manner of presentation is also intended as a sign: that the classical proportions are not here to be taken literally, or else to be taken so literally as to undermine their overt sense. The building does not in fact complete itself in congruency with the classical expectations which it announces. The corners are voided of structure. There is no closure at the foot of the walls, between panels, at the corners, nor between wall and roof. All these junctions are voided. Internally the surface of metal is never allowed to complete itself. Discrepancies and gaps continually reveal the world beyond the confinement of the building.

2.42 Divisible by 2 is further divided into the following harmonic proportions which operate simultaneously: thirds (the proportion of double door to width of elevation, A:A:A), fourths (the aluminum frame, A:B:B:A), fifths (the external surface of the panels, A:B:C:B:A).

2.43 Also present in the doors and in the facade are atonal rhythms (panel-door-door-panel, A-D-E-A). The machinery of the building is allowed to register on the exterior without obeying the symmetry demanded by classical harmonies.

2.44 The building is simultaneously harmonic and discordant, classical and disturbed. This disturbance in the classical points to the sense of the interior where only the discrepant dimensions of male and female are used in a single space, a hall of metonyms for the body.

2.5 The Floor

2.51 The floor is made of clear, shiny high-polymer resin. In the resin are set the devices of organization, pleasure and figural beauty from the city — lipstick, shaving mirrors, razors, cigarettes, signs, money. These float in the transparency of the resin which is poured over black tar and sparsely filled with straw. The floor is a metaphor of the conjunctions of city and countryside.

2.52 The floor is a failure, an architectural failure. There are two senses in which this failure can be understood. The first sense of failure is constructional. The chemical process of the resin killed and removed the color from the intended composition of the floor. The floor would have been entirely different had the splashes of color originally placed within it survived. We do not know how this would have read. It was intended that the now too explicit nature of the metaphor should pass over into a more abstract and uncontrolled experience of wild flashes of color. Intense color had been excluded from the building, and only allowed to enter as reflection. This error in the pouring of the resin, this killing of the color, could perhaps have been avoided. The second sense is an irreparable failure. It was a strategic mistake to treat the floor as metaphor, rather than, say, a more complex transaction between the imported material of flowers or glass and the structure of the floor itself.

2.6 The Roof

2.61 The roof functions as a diffuser of light which is then subsequently reflected on the interior to a very high degree. The effect is equivalent to extending the resonance of a chord in music. The feeling is even and extremely light, even on a dark day. It also helps to create the effect that the interior is the outside. In sunshine, direct light invades the building from the corners and the eaves in an uncontrolled manner, registering itself directly in the interior. Thus the architecture of the room, itself very deliberated, is consciously contingent upon the nature of light at any particular moment.

2.62 The gutters pour the rain water at the corners of the building where the column has been voided. In the rain the classical columns are replaced by water. Only water can occupy the corner.

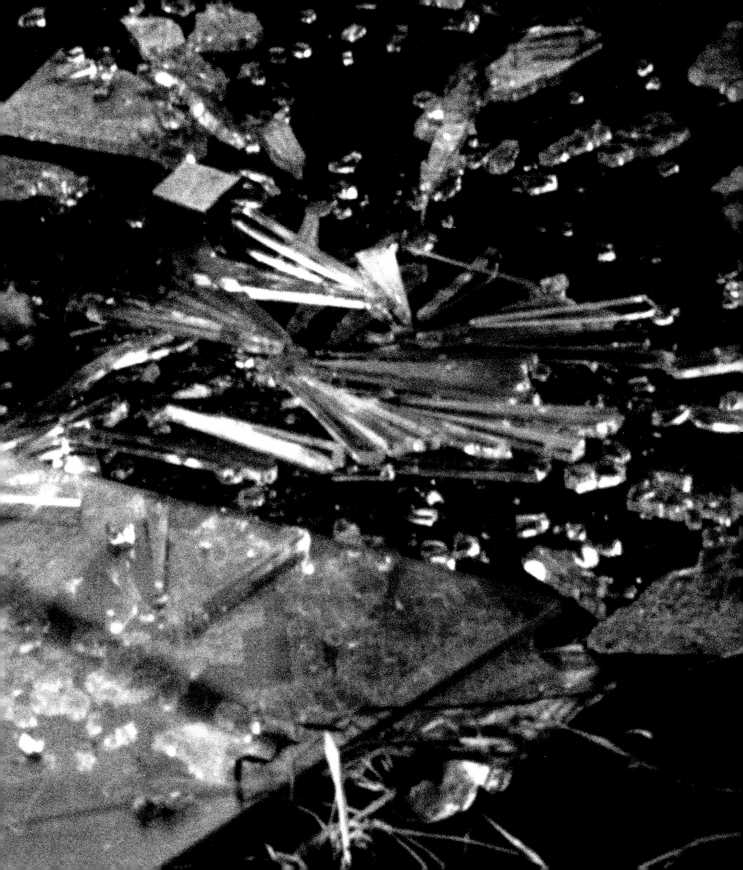

3 Body and Building

3.1 The Building in the Round

3.11 Looked at frontally the building appears to be a solid. Looked at from askew the building reveals a void-like nature. It is essentially ambiguous. Or rather, it presents a double aspect, alternately solid and void. In a certain way of thinking the building is not really a building, for it presents all the effects of surface in isolation, and the mass usually associated with a surface has been retracted. The building is articulated as a series of surfaces, its volume has been picked apart mechanically. On the interior the space leaks away. Alternations of solid and void abound in the building which always tries to hide its own body, by retracting its mass and showing only its surfaces.

3.12 "The problems of life are insoluble on the surface and can only be solved in depth. They are insoluble in surface dimensions."4 Here again architecture, the mechanism by which depth is created, is used unknowingly as metaphor by a philosopher. When speaking architecturally, is his statement true?

3.13 The interior of the building has an external aspect. It is like being outside. The interior may be read as urban space. In one sense the doors are ineffectual for they do not make a transition from outside to inside. The inside is incomplete and too overly charged with a sense of the public to be regarded as an internal space.

3.14 The body of the building, as initiated by the plan and its proportions, is not fulfilled. The corners are missing, the walls are often void, surfaces are not allowed to complete themselves.

3.2 Experience

3.21 It was imagined there would be three phases of experience of the building. 1. On approach: a generation of expectations, associated with lavatory doors, of ease of access and a separation of the sexes. In addition, upon approach a betrayal in the composition of the doors that these expectations are not going to be met. 2. At the threshold: an arresting of the subject, literally a stopping of forward movement, and an arresting of initial expectations, achieved by the structure of passage through the doors and by the presentation of an illusion of frontality on the interior. 3. In the interior: a conjunction with the other sex and a form of aimless wandering given the discrepant dimensionality of the interior panels, and a fascination with their difficult reflectivity.

3.22 These three phases of experience are correlated with stages of transformation in the subject from user to performer: expectation, disturbance, experience without expectation. But the mapping is not direct, linear or causal, for each stage subsequent to the approach is betrayed in earlier stages, and the building may be understood therefore without entering.

3.23 What in fact happens in the experience of the building? It is somewhat different from the above. Or is it merely that an anticipatory account merely does not go far or deep enough? The account is most incomplete as regards the experience of the interior. Once inside, a person moves as expected somewhat tentatively into the interior space. Having opened the aluminum panel that obstructs entry, and having encountered the facade which opposes entry, a person moves forward into the space. The body is placed in opposition to an interior facade. But the scale of the facade and its presentations of bodily metonyms are such that a person tends to back away. In backing away from one facade, a person confronts another, and quickly backs away again. One becomes aware of an extreme difficulty in placing one's own body in the space of the building. Where to be? How to stand? The difficulty of standing. Here? There? In this difficulty and in the motion created by its indeterminacy there arises a search to try to find a place to stand. The building seems at first to refuse the stasis of the body, at least until what is seen through the eye can be accounted for in the recollection or memory of one's experience of the building as it accumulates.

3.24 But the movements of search tend to lead one toward the center of the building, and, because the center has been voided compositionally, it is unbearable to stand there. At the center all four facades press their case upon the subject. In general a person moves away from the center toward the edge, so close to a wall that its representational effects are no longer within the compass of the eye and are therefore ineffective as presentations. As a consequence movement in the building tends to be peripheral and rotational. In this rotational movement, the experience of the building is radically changed. Instead of reading the interior panels statically as discrete objects, each a metonym for a door and consequently a metonym for a body, the act of rotational movement leads to a concatenation of lines and figures. In rotation, in passing by the panels, a sequential rhythm of discordant dimensions is created, a music of discrepancy. No harmonic dimensions are registered on the interior.

3.25 With the presence of more than one person in the building at the same time, each obeys a similar pattern of experience as described above. But approaching the center becomes more difficult in the presence of another person. The rotational movement induced by the building tends to occur more quickly. Persons move with regard to one another, the experience of self as a mirror of the presence of the other. They tend to settle in asymmetrical compositions, away from the center, usually in one quadrant of the building.

3.26 In both accounts the experience of the building is rendered self-conscious, if not painfully so, such that a person is made perpetually aware of movement and position. Can this self-consciousness, which radically transforms the experience of the building from that of user to performer, be said to be the conduit of the political in architectural experience? But, given that such reflexive experience depends on a play with conventions buried deep within the ordinary, itself seen as sedimented or a convention/pathological metaphor, can it be that such acts (if effective? Is this one effective? I don't know.) have a

half-life? Within different historical regimes of the ordinary, perhaps they cannot be read? If the history of the ordinary progresses, changing its conventionality, then perhaps the experience of prior reflexive gestures can no longer be had.

3.27 Think of Nelson Goodman's question, not "What is art?" but "When is art?" If architecture is not subject to time, the experience of architecture certainly is. But this paradox only points more to the dark body of architecture, for what is it in architecture that survives the changing regimes of reading? What persists? What endures?

3.28 The building concerns the placement of the subject, and this as a political act. Architecture as the placement of the subject. Positions.

3.29 The complexity of these arguments notwithstanding, the ordinary person is always capable of sensing the emotions of a work of architecture, of tracing its circuits of feeling and knowing when something is rightly made or not. Sensibility, not argumentation, is our best guide to a work. Which is not to say that people always in fact do this, merely that they are always capable of it. That is to say people are capable of an extraordinary intuitive knowledge about the formation of an architectural object. It may come quickly and completely to their eyes. And yet this skill is not always exercised, perhaps cannot be always exercised?

"Architecture has always represented the prototype of a work of art the reception of which is consummated by a collectivity in a state of distraction. The laws of its reception are most instructive."

W Benjamin, "The Work of Art in the Age of Mechanical Reproduction" in *Illuminations*, New York, 1969, p 239

4 L Wittgenstein, *Culture and Value*, Chicago, 1980, p 74e

3.3 On Interpretation

3.31 What would it be to experience a building without purpose? "Architecture is a *gesture*. Not every purposive movement of the human body is a gesture. And no more is every building designed for a purpose architecture."[5]

3.32 Interpretations of architecture construct a verbal paralogy of the building. The experience of architecture is lifted into the sense of words. The verbal construct simultaneously operates two relations with the object of its sense. First, by a technique of reference, the verbal construct points away from its own object, the word, to the object of its sense, here the building. Second, the verbal construct is made, lifting one sense (architecture) into another (words) so that it points back to the body of the building, but obliquely.

3.33 A tension arises between the apparently autonomous logics of grammatical and architectural form. In as much as a verbal interpretation makes sense of the experience of a building, so there is a stand-off created between the logical form of words and that of building. The former cannot be used to direct or instruct the latter. No line of instrumental thought is possible between the two.

3.34 Without the acknowledgment of the operation of formative transactions between building and word, the logic of architecture subsequently collapses into the paradox of representation, that is, the nonnegotiable division between the autonomous senses of self-relatedness and the open, transactional modes of reference between modes of sense-making, between internalized and externalizing sense.

3.35 The puzzle between the autonomy of a work of art and its external references is an old one. Mostly theories of the artwork must acknowledge both the formalist's project and also the project of the meaning-theorist or reader and the cultural theorist.

3.36 Both projects can only coalesce when the false puzzles of representation are excluded as a project of understanding or making the artwork.

5 L Wittgenstein, *Culture and Value*, Chicago, 1980, p 42

4 Architectural Afterthoughts

4.1   The building is intended merely as surface and space. The building tries to present the spatial effect of surface while simultaneously retracting the sense of mass. In this sense, of the withdrawal of mass, the building is not a building? Architecturally this necessitates the presence of the frame, and the consequence that the presence of the frame must be minimized, and yet be structurally integral to the presentation of surfaces.

4.2   The use of articulation as a means of mental display is related to the project of transparency, at least in the philosophical sense of laying bare, of revealing all, as if the project of making evident is itself a form of honesty. As in Rousseau, a transparency so intense that even men's hearts may be seen.

4.3   Notice the difference between transparency as a metaphor for a philosophical description of our subjective condition and as a more literal architectural condition, transparency as a phenomenological property in a building. In this building the two are not correlated as they are in the modernist project of transparency.

4.4   Each sense of transparency is no guarantor of the presence of the other. Transparency in building is no guarantee of transparency of experience.

4.5   The project of the eye finds a limitation. The mental extensions that can be made from the condition of human finitude provoke a disjunction between what can be known and what can be seen. This disjunction is the opportunity of knowledge and also the necessity of skepticism.

4.6   Thus the phenomenon of the building finds a limit. The qualities of architecture become disjoined from the architectural revelations about self, other and the conditions of community. The architectural project of transparency cannot therefore be a *sine qua non* of the ideal conditions for an open society. The two conditions are not isomorphs of one another: they do not follow from one another in conditions of necessity.

4.7   The architectural technique of this building is an exercise in the opacity of surface and an investigation of how opacity is presented to the subject as a space-defining and experience-giving *techne*.

John Hejduk **Commentary**

The pages that follow are a commentary
by John Hejduk on John Whiteman's text.
Hejduk's comments are numbered in
accordance with the original.
Extracts from John Whiteman's text appear
in the left hand column and have been
enclosed in quotation marks.
The dictionary definitions have been
reprinted by permission from Webster's
Third New International Dictionary
© 1986 by Merriam-Webster Inc.,
publisher of the Merriam-Webster ®
dictionaries.

RELATION BETWEEN ARCHITECTURE AND POLITICS

Letter from Austria . . .

the destruction of art
the destruction of architecture
the attempted destruction of thought

the fabrication of art
the fabrication of architecture
the fabrication of thought

the necessity of building small
the social contract
the mobility of structures
the program . . . the key?

RELATIONSHIP BETWEEN TEXT AND ___BUILDING___
ARCHITECTURE

¹**as·sas·sin** \ə'sasᵊn, -saas- *sometimes* -sin\ *n* -s [ML *assassinus*, fr. Ar *hashshāshīn*, pl. of *hashshāsh* one who smokes or chews hashish, hashish addict, fr. *hashīsh* hemp, hashish] **1** *usu cap* : one of a secret order of Muslims that at the time of the Crusades terrorized Christians and other enemies by secret murder committed under the influence of hashish **2** : MURDERER; *esp* : one that murders either for hire or from fanatic adherence to a cause

destroyed by
fluid
explosion
heat
melt down
remains of
ashes
burnt wood
melted metal
frame collapse
assassins
in the night
night prowlers
night/light
odor of ashes
odor of liquid
odor of hate
the taste of ash

in·ter·ro·gate \-rə‚gāt, *usu* -ād·+V\ *vb* -ED/-ING/-S [L *interrogatus*, past part, of *interrogare*, fr. *inter-* + *rogare* to ask, request — more at RIGHT] *vt* **1** : to question typically with formality, command, and thoroughness for full information and circumstantial detail ⟨∼ a witness⟩ **2** *obs* : to ask questions about **3** : to examine in detail : research into the causes, reasons, nature of ⟨modern potters ∼ in their laboratories the glazes used in ancient China —C.E. Montague⟩ ∼ *vi* : to ask questions of someone : conduct an examination ⟨frank I will respond as you ∼ —Robert Browning⟩ **syn** see ASK

0   Text and Building

0.2   Interrogate . . .

the torturer's weapon
a word for the wearers
of jack/boot.

A fear full word.
In the mind text and building

are inseparable.

0.3   Thought recognizes no difference

of medium.

0.4   "dependency of building on word"

he honors his word
he gives his word of honor

"false signs on the doors"
                    English translation

Men
Women
men/wo/men

1   Beginnings and Motivations

1.1   Architecture can not render
            in art *to render* is a negative attempt.
        "architecture itself as political"

a futile task

Politics always gets in the way.
Architects can be caught in
                        the power system

not architecture.

In many cases, machines can be

considered political.

Recently works are taking on
                    machine characteristics,

a bad omen?

Some architecture can illicit dread.

¹dread \\'dred\ *vb* -ED/-ING/-S [ME *dreden*, fr. OE *drǣdan;* akin to OS ant*drādan* to fear, dread, OHG in*trātan*] *vt*   **1 a** : to fear greatly : be in terror of ⟨a burned child ~s the fire⟩   **b** *archaic* : to stand in awe of : REVERENCE   **2** : to anticipate with fear of evil, pain, or trouble : look forward to with apprehensiveness : feel great anxiety about ⟨they ~ change, lest it should make matters worse —G.B.Shaw⟩ ~ *vi* : to be very apprehensive or fearful ⟨~ not, neither be afraid of them —Deut 1: 29 (AV)⟩

²dread \"'\ *n* -S [ME *drede, dred*, fr. *dreden*, v.]   **1 a** : great fear esp. in the face of impending evil : fearful apprehension of danger : anticipatory terror ⟨looked forward with ~ to the night alone in the dark farmhouse —Sherwood Anderson⟩ ⟨~ of insecurity⟩   **b** *archaic* : reverential or respectful fear : AWE   **2** : a person or thing regarded with fear or awe ⟨the days of wooden ships and wooden homes, when fire was an omnipresent ~ —F.W.Saunders⟩   **3** [trans. of Dan & G *angst*] : ANXIETY 3 **syn** see FEAR

1.12   I never use the word power.

                          The above is a contradiction.

1.15   Architecture also has to do with the

                                                    collapse of space
                                                    collapse of distance

              see   Jay Fellows,
                        The Failing Distance,
                        The Autobiographical Impulse
                        in John Ruskin, Baltimore, 1975

1.17   I am worried for Wittgenstein.
              His words, always being quoted
              have the tendency to undermine
              the earth below his grave.
              A *de-stabilization* is taking place.

                          Everything need not be

                                              translated into words.

1.18   We can not enter a building

                                                    without a heart
                                                    without heart.

1.19   Medium is a dead-end.

                          I am *nowhere.*

1.2 Architecture and Human Difference

1.21   There is no such thing as neutrality

in architecture

it participates in the differences

of life.

1.22   Yes,
"architecture...as an inscription of the subjectivity"

1.31   Architecture gives us what it wants.
There is no reason not
to speak to object/architecture

with/in love.

"dominance over an object"

what a sad thought

1.32   I prefer subject of our desire.

1.33   We have the banality of evil all around us.

Somehow the word corrupt always pops up
with the word political.

It's an age old condition.

1.34   ¹lav·a·to·ry \ˈlavə͵tōre, -tȯr-, -ri\ n -ES [ME *lavatorie*, fr. ML
lavatorium, fr. L *lavatus* (past part. of *lavare* to wash) + *-orium*] 1 :
a basin or other vessel for washing: as **a** : PISCINA **b** : a water basin
in a sacristy **2** : a ritual washing of the hands by a celebrant of the
Eucharist : LAVABO 1a **3** : a place for washing: as **a** : a room with
conveniences for washing the hands and face and usu. with one or
more toilets **b** : a fixed bowl or basin with running water and
drainpipe for washing the hands and face **c** : a place, trough, or tub
in which bodies are washed before burial **4** : **WATER CLOSET, TOI-
LET**

1.35   For the patient of a urologist

lavatory

is an important word.

1.36   Graffiti in Europe is political; in America, personal.
Like stairs
the lavatories are integral,

difficult to escape.

1.37 "In the banality of the lavatory door is subsumed the major system of devices by which architecture is appropriated in(to) life. The sign indicates function. The door, itself a metonym of the body, indicates passage and, in conjunction with the sign, ease of access. Door and sign together indicated a security if not a certainty. The threat of the other side of the door is nullified by the exterior sign arousing a confidence of use, and in turn creating new threats of 'the other'. The ordinary door, upon opening, places the subject at the threshold of a room which by optical projection s/he can grasp as intelligible. A visual map is made of the room in a single glance. The projection once made, the architecture thus appropriated, the room can be used in accordance with its function. Nothing in the architecture is to trouble the subject further. The architecture is exhausted, no longer needed. It can be left behind, forgotten."

1.4 The plucking out and the singular appropriation of loved things and the consequent closing down of usage. The closing down of certain letters of a vocabulary. As an analogy...as if someone takes or appropriates out of a collective vocabulary the letter "E", that is, the appropriator, by insisting on appropriating for his or her *singular* use, simply takes out of circulation the possible use by others of what had once been a universal detail. This could be seen as the loss of a limb moving negatively to the non-functioning of a vital organ and its eventual disappearance...atrophy.

1.51 "disfigured" is a loaded word particularly within the conventional understanding

of architecture.

cal·i·brate \'kalə,brāt, *usu* -ād·+V\ *vt* -ED/-ING/-S [*caliber* + -*ate*] **1 a** *obs* : to ascertain the caliber of (as a thermometer tube) **b** : to determine or mark the capacity or the graduations of or to rectify the graduations of (as a graduated measuring instrument) **c** : to standardize (as a measuring instrument) by determining the deviation from standard esp. so as to ascertain the proper correction factors **2** : to determine by actual firing the corrections in range or elevation settings required to make (a piece of artillery) fire uniformly with a standard or reference piece

1.56 "the building as an architectural machine"

the argument is joined.

1.6 The user and the performer are in fact, the same person.

1.62 deceit and counterfeit

one subject
one object

1.63 "ordination"

co-ordination

51

2 Verbal Incursions

Incursion is an aggressive term.

2.1 "The doors."

> **door** \'dō(ə)r, -ȯ(ə)r,-ōə,-ȯ(ə\ *n* -s [ME *dor*, fr. OE, door, gate & ME *dure*, fr. OE *duru*; akin to OHG *tor* & *turi* door, gate, ON *dyrr*, Goth *daur*, L *fores*, Gk *thyra*, Skt *dvār*] **1 a** : a movable piece of firm material or a structure supported usu. along one side and swinging on pivots or hinges, sliding along a groove, rolling up and down, revolving as one of four leaves, or folding like an accordion by means of which an opening may be closed or kept open for passage into or out of a building, room, or other covered enclosure or a car, airplane, elevator, or other vehicle — see **KALAMEIN DOOR, PANEL DOOR** **b** : a similar part by which access is prevented or allowed to the contents of a repository, cabinet, vault, or refrigeration or combustion chamber **2 a** : an opening in a wall of a building, room, or a side or rear of a vehicle by which to go in or out : **DOORWAY** **b** : one of two openings 3½ ft. wide in the wall of a court-tennis court between the first and second gallery **3 a** : a means of access, admittance, participation, or enjoyment ⟨the opening of our ~*s* to all the distressed peoples of Asia —M.R.Cohen⟩ ⟨leaving the ~ open for a settlement⟩ ⟨opening with the magic of storytelling the ~*s* to the world's great treasure house of literature —Nancy K. Hosking⟩ **b** : an opening or route that suggests or resembles a door in giving physical access, entrance, or exit ⟨this pass was the ~ through which the invaders poured into the doomed country⟩ ⟨slipped into Switzerland by almost the last remaining ~ out of France —Robert Payne⟩ **4 a** : one of the entranceways to buildings in a row; *esp* : one facing on a street ⟨he resides three ~*s* beyond the church⟩ ⟨living next ~ to you⟩ **b** : one's home and immediate family or one's personal knowledge and experience ⟨striving to keep scandal from his ~⟩ ⟨this fact was not left to Japanese research to discover: it was brought to their ~ —A.M. Young⟩ **5** : a gateway at the threshold of some supernatural realm or giving escape from the normal human state ⟨the old statesman lingered for several weeks at death's ~⟩

The new space is the space of

the threshold.

Doors are either opened or closed
or locked.

2.11 The Alhambra makes clear
the entry through two openings
without doors.
The choice, as always,

of good and evil.

2.12   The sexes are introduced.
But only two of the sexes.
Where are the other four?
The idea of the architecture of betrayal.
Door handles, the bruising of the flesh
architecture which punishes through detail.

2.14   What is the sex of a building?
What is the sex of an architect?

The inflation of the *American Graphic Standards*

from 1943 to 1968.

"marked, scratched, burned, inscribed"
Words of the penal lawyer.
A body manual for the prison guard.

The introduction of the word "composition".

2.15   At what date was the usage of framing
around door openings commenced?
At what date was the frame
around paintings commenced?
"occupied by the neutrality of. . ."

Neutral. . .Neuter
Architecture can be female/male
Architect Male/female

Photographs are independent.
They tend to capture the un-seeable.

2.17   the guillotine

"metal arrests"   mental arrest   the brain captured
the soul evaporating

2.19 "the space of the body"

infinite

Celebration of the wall.
Mutual distance/difference/between male female.
Mutual dependence
structural marriage
structural mirage

2.2 The Plan

2.21   Is there not a redundancy in using
            the word perfect in perfect square?

            I want to *touch* the square
            particularly its corners.

2.22   The space of the city is one/many.

man·da·la \\'mǝndǝlǝ\ *n* -s [Skt *mandala* circle] : a graphic mystic
symbol of the universe that is typically in the form of a circle enclosing
a square and often bearing symmetrically arranged representations of
deities and is used chiefly in Hinduism and Buddhism as an aid to
meditation

            Aim. . .less

2.24   "hidden by the door"

2.26   "s/he"

            the dominance of the "he"

                                                                    a problem

2.27   **il·lu·sion** \ǝ'lüzhǝn *also* ǝl'yü-\ *n* -s [ME *illusioun*, fr.
            MF *illusion*, fr.
            LL *illusion-, illusio*, fr. L, action of mocking, jeering, fr. *illusus* (past
            part. of *illudere* to mock or jeer at, fr. *in-* ²in- + *ludere* to play, mock,
            jeer) + *ion-, -io* -ion — more at LUDICROUS] **1 a** *obs* : the action of
            deceiving or attempting to deceive   **b** (1) : the state or fact of being
            intellectually deceived or deluded or misled by others or by oneself
            either intentionally or unintentionally in such a way as to have false
            impressions or ideas marked by the attribution of more to something
            or less to something than is actually the case : MISAPPREHENSION,
            MISCONCEPTION, DELUSION, FANCY ⟨the happy ~s of youth⟩   (2) :
            an instance of such deception or delusion ⟨a dreamy life that was filled
            with one ~ after another⟩   **2 a** (1) : a misleading image presented to
            the vision : false show; *specif* : APPARITION ⟨these were all an ~ and a
            phantasma, a thing that appeared, but did not really exist —F.W.
            Robertson⟩   (2) : something that deceives or deludes or misleads
            intellectually in such a way as to produce false impressions or ideas that
            exaggerate or minimize reality or that attribute existence to what does
            not exist or nonexistence to what does exist ⟨most modern great men
            are mere ~s sprung out of a national hunger for greatness —Sherwood
            Anderson⟩   **b** (1) : perception of something objectively existing in
            such a way as to cause or permit misinterpretation of its actual nature
            either because of the ambiguous qualities of the thing perceived or
            because of the personal characteristics of the one perceiving or because
            of both factors ⟨heat rays shimmering on the road produced the ~ of
            pools of water⟩ ⟨the horizontal lines cause an optical ~, making the
            object appear in a different position from what it really is in —Richard
            Jefferies⟩

            "rotational"

                is a questionable word

                                                        over   in
                                                        _____
                                                        used   architecture

2.3   The Interior

2.31   encyclical on harmonic proportions
             ecclesiastical laws on allowability

2.32   The moment when Orpheus begins
             his turn

                                                    all is lost

2.33   *circular perspective*

       "concantenations across different reflective surfaces"
                              a prayer

2.34   "discrepant dimensions between men and women"

2.35   Orson Welles' *Shanghai Lady*
                                  One of the few real cubist films
             The threat to one of multiple

                                                    extinction.

2.4   The Facade

2.41   "The facade departs from a series of classical harmonies. These are presented in the same 'sign-
       like' manner as the signs on the doors. Their direct manner of presentation is also intended as a
       sign: that the classical proportions are not here to be taken literally, or else to be taken so literally
       as to undermine their overt sense. The building does not in fact complete itself in congruency with
       the classical expectations which it announces. The corners are voided of structure. There is no
       closure at the foot of the walls, between panels, at the corners, between wall and roof. All these
       junctions are voided. Internally the surface of metal is never allowed to complete itself. Discrepan-
       cies and gaps continually reveal the world beyond the confinement of the building."

2.42   see   R Wittkower, *Architectural Principles in the Age of
                                     Humanism.* New York, 1971
             Difficulty of getting to "C"

2.43   "A-D-E-A"   I-D-E-A

2.44   The disturbance of the vague mirrors.

2.5 The Floor

2.51   Something is left out in the listing.

2.52

fail·ure \ˈfālyə(r)\ *n* -s [alter. (influenced by *-ure*) of earlier *failer*, fr. AF *failer*, fr. OF *faillir* to fail — more at **FAIL**] **1 a** : omission of performance of an action or task; *esp* : neglect of an assigned, expected, or appropriate action ⟨the mechanic's ∼ to adjust the brake⟩ ⟨the ∼ of students to write complete sentences⟩ ⟨the scout's ∼ to rejoin the party⟩ **b** : the fact of a certain action or process not having occurred : the fact of nonoccurrence ⟨∼ of the water to pass through the pipe⟩ ⟨the ∼ of the drug to have a harmful effect⟩ **2** : want of success : lack of satisfactory performance or effect ⟨the ∼ of the attack on the fort⟩ ⟨the ∼ of the candidate in the election⟩ **3** *obs* : **FAILING, LAPSE** **4 a** : **DEFICIENCY, LACK** : the fact of being cumulatively inadequate or not matching hopes or expectations ⟨the crop ∼s brought on near famine⟩ **b** : **ABSENCE, NONEXISTENCE** ⟨through ∼ of heirs, most of the state societies had disintegrated —A.F.Harlow⟩ **c** : marked weakening : the fact of becoming exhausted or enfeebled : **DETERIORA-TION** ⟨any impairment or ∼ of his bodily vigor through sickness or age —J.G.Frazer⟩ **d** *med* : inability to perform a vital function ⟨heart ∼⟩ **e** : a collapsing, fracturing, or giving way under stress : inability of a material or structure to fulfill an intended purpose **5 a** : **BANKRUPTCY** ⟨the ∼ of the company⟩ ⟨the ∼ of a friend whose note he had endorsed⟩ **b** : a venture financially unsuccessful ⟨although a contribution to literature, the play was a box-office ∼⟩ **6** : a person or thing that has failed ⟨people who were either ∼s or had had no ambitions —Louis Bromfield⟩ ⟨the war against the confederation was a ∼⟩ **7 a** : the fact of failing in a test or course **b** : a failing grade **c** : a student who has failed

The de-foliation, the de-chlorophylling

of architecture.

"irreparable failure"

death

2.6 The Roof

2.61   "extending the resonance of a chord"

architecture

2.62   Liquid Faction

3　Body and Building

3.11　"leaks away"

　　　　　　　　　　　. . .an autopsy

3.12　　　Conventional description,
　　　　　the brain hides the body.

　　　　　　　　　　　　　　　the surface en lightens.

3.13　　　From the outside man's organs

　　　　　　　　　　　　　　　cannot be seen.

3.14　　　A building in crisis?

3.2　Experience

3.21　"It was imagined there would be three phases of experience in the building. 1 On approach: a generation of expectations, associated with lavatory doors, of ease of access and a separation of the sexes. In addition, upon approach a betrayal in the composition of the doors that these expectations are not going to be met. 2 At the threshold: an arresting of the subject, literally a stopping of forward movement, and an arresting of initial expectations, achieved by the structure of passage through the doors and by the presentation of an illusion of frontality on the interior. 3 In the interior: a conjunction with the other sex and a form of aimless wandering given the discrepant dimensionality of the interior panels, and a fascination with their difficult reflectivity."

3.22　　　Mapping
　　　　　until recently was an honorable discipline.
　　　　　Under siege
　　　　　its precision is hated by the terrorist.

3.23　　　Building held to account.

　　　　　Maximum compression produces maximum extension.

3.25　　　Ariadne and the Bull

　　　　　　　　　　　　　　　same faith
　　　　　　　　　　　　　　　opposite direction
　　　　　　　　　room for a sexual encounter

3.26   I am not a user.
        I am not a performer.

        Sediment
        no life/half-life/full life

                                                        Nature Morte

        Architecture addresses dead time.

3.28   Political acts tend to disregard the subject.

3.29   To make right.   What right?

        It must come to their souls.
        The essentiality of the intuitive.

        The angel of Benjamin flying
        backward into the future
        carrying the dead in its wake.

3.3 On Interpretation

3.31   Program is necessary.

3.32   The pleasures of interpretation.

3.36   The impossibility of completing
        a puzzle without all of the pieces.

4   Architectural Afterthoughts

4.1   "The building is intended merely as surface and space. The building tries to present
the spatial effect of surface while simultaneously retracting the sense of mass."

        In making man God covered the bones
        and whiteness too.

4.2   The opacity of transparency.

                                      One can only sense the heart

4.4   I feel my thoughts inside.

4.5   conjunction

4.6   Literal transparency   phenomenal transparency
                                                          Rowe/Slutzky

        The fogs of Oslo
        Chilling to the bone
        The austerity of severities

I WAS UNABLE TO SEE JOHN WHITEMAN'S
PAVILION   IN AUSTRIA
BUT I SEE IT . . . .

A STRUCTURE WAS BURNT DOWN

Some/one told me that John Whiteman
was doing a structure/construction

        in Austria.

I was interested to know it.

Later . . .

Then I heard . . .

        that it was built.

Then I heard . . .

        that it was destroyed
        in Austria.

Then I heard

        past sounds

and thought of other destructions.
For some reason I was not surprised

        I was saddened.

Then I became angry
by the vicious violence done to a work

        of architecture.

Images arose of figures in the night

        destroying
        an architect's work.

I was not surprised that this happened

        in Austria.

The structure was fire destroyed.

        It was burned
        and it was melted.

Yet, the thought of John Whiteman
is indestructible.
Although the structure/construction

        was horribly burnt down

the architect's thought cannot be

        burnt down.